REMARKABLE JOURNEYS
The Story of Jules Verne

REMARKABLE JOURNEYS
The Story of Jules Verne

William Schoell

620 South Elm Street, Suite 223
Greensboro, North Carolina   27406
http://www.morganreynolds.com

REMARKABLE JOURNEYS: THE STORY OF JULES VERNE

Illustrations are courtesy of the Library of Congress, unless otherwise noted.

Library of Congress Cataloging-in-Publication Data

Schoell, William.
　Remarkable journeys : the story of Jules Verne / William Schoell.
　　p. cm.
Summary: A biography of the nineteenth-century Frenchman whose childhood
love of literature, science, and adventure, along with his vivid
imagination, led him to become a highly successful science fiction
author.
Includes bibliographical references and index.
　ISBN 1-883846-92-7
　1. Verne, Jules, 1828-1905—Juvenile literature. 2. Authors,
French—19th century—Biography—Juvenile literature. [1. Verne, Jules,
1828-1905. 2. Authors, French.]　I. Title.
　PQ2469.Z5 S36 2002
　843'.8—dc21

2002002016

Printed in the United States of America
First Edition

Contents

Jules Verne, 1876

Chapter One

"In My Imagination"

It was the boats that most fascinated young Jules Verne. Beginning at an early age, the future writer yearned to see beyond the confines of the small port city of Nantes, France. Nantes spread over both banks of the Loire River and was only forty miles inland from the Atlantic Ocean. Young Jules imagined what foreign, exotic ports beyond the Brittany coast would look like, before he began imagining what places where no one had ever been—the depths of the sea, the moon, even the inside of the earth itself—would look like. The everyday world was not enough to satisfy him; he wanted to venture into unknown worlds and make them vivid in his mind. Later he would want to make these images vivid in the minds of his readers.

But at first there were only the boats. Jules Gabriel Verne was born in France on February 8, 1828. He and his family lived on Ile Feydeau, an island in the Loire

River that belonged to the city. A cobblestone main street ran from one end of the island to the other and there were beaches on each tip. Surrounding the island was a *quai* (dock) where many small boats were moored. Beyond the quai, the river rushed past on its way to the ocean.

When Jules's mother, Sophie Verne, took her son shopping, he paid more attention to the boats in the Loire River than he did to the bakeries, fish markets, and vegetable stands. On trips to the mainland with his parents and brother, Paul, Jules loved to go to the docks and watch the larger ships in the harbor. He knew the ships had sailed from all over the world and they awakened dreams within him of wonderful adventures in far-off places and whispered of an unconventional life at sea.

Jules's father, Pierre Verne, was a struggling lawyer. The Vernes lived in Pierre's mother's house and dreamed of the day when they could have their own home. Pierre did not have the imagination that Jules did, but he did love to read adventure stories to his sons: Sir Walter Scott's *Ivanhoe* and James Fenimore Cooper's *The Last of the Mohicans* were two favorites. Jules had a close relationship with his brother, Paul, who was a year younger. They spent their free hours exploring the island and discussing the books their father read to them. After he learned to read himself, Jules became a voracious reader.

Sophie Henriette Verne

Pierre Verne

Jules's uncle, Francis de Châteaubourg, who was an artist and had traveled a great deal, also nourished his imagination. He passed on many of his stories to his nephews. Some of the stories were tall tales, but Jules and Paul hung on to every word. In a favorite yarn, their uncle claimed that it was a member of his family who actually discovered the Northwest Passage and not an Englishman. Every story added to Jules's desire to somehow get on one of those boats sailing out of the Nantes port and see the strange, exciting sights of the world. Every cargo taken off the ships—coffee, sugar cane— had come from *somewhere* else. Jules thought it would be great to go *somewhere* some day!

As well as adventure, Jules had an early interest in science and literature. In 1833, when Jules was five, the telegraph was invented, and he pestered his Aunt and Uncle de Châteaubourg to buy a toy version for him and Paul to play with. One of the first letters the small boy wrote was to ask his relatives to make sure they brought a telegraph with them when they visited. But even the invention of the telegraph could not make Jules forget about his boats and all they represented.

He was haunted by a story about one of his school-teachers, a lady who claimed that her husband had sailed off thirty years before and never returned. Jules wondered what had become of the man, and what kind of adventures he may have had.

As the years progressed, Pierre Verne's law practice

prospered, and the family grew. Three sisters joined Jules and Paul: Anna, Marie, and Mathilde. They moved from the island to their own house in Nantes proper. There, Jules spent even more time on the docks, watching the boats and the sailors with envy and anticipation. Everywhere he went, Jules carried with him a note pad or copybook in which he made sketches and jotted down his thoughts and impressions.

He and Paul were thrilled the first time they saw a steamboat with its giant, swirling paddle wheel and smokestack belching fumes. Jules also loved the stage-coach or "omnibus," which was a very large carriage pulled by two horses. The horses of the first omnibus Jules saw were white, as was the uniform of the coach-man, and the paint on the carriage itself. It became known as the "White Lady." If steam could power a boat, Jules wondered, could it also some day power a carriage?

When Jules was nine, he and Paul were enrolled in the Seminary of Saint Donatien, a boarding school for boys. Jules was not especially interested in his studies. Years later he would say, "Studious children invariably turn into half-witted grown-ups." He enjoyed athlet-ics—and dreaming. He discovered the fun of walking on stilts and towering over his classmates. He practiced on his stilts at the summer home his father had bought in nearby Chantenay, which at that time was not part of Nantes. The summer home had a garden and hills to play on and was located on the Loire River where Jules could see his beloved boats sailing by.

Jules wanted to visit Paris. It might not have been possible for him to sail to distant ports, which he prefered, but Paris seemed within reach. Paul confided that he hoped to be the captain of a ship when he was older. Jules cared less about being a captain than about being a simple passenger going to some place interesting. Soon, he almost got his wish.

Jules went alone to Nantes one afternoon and headed directly to the port where he struck up a conversation with a boy about his age who was sitting on the dock having his lunch. Jules was thrilled to learn that he was the cabin boy for the sailing ship *Coralie*, which was anchored in the river. The cabin boy told Jules that the ship was bound for the West Indies.

While the cabin boy was matter-of-fact about life on a ship, Jules was so excited he could barely contain himself. He asked numerous questions about what a cabin boy was supposed to do on the voyage. A cabin boy was given room and board, he learned, and a little money. The work did not sound too hard, and Jules had saved up his allowance. He told the cabin boy that he would give him more money than he would earn on the voyage if he would let Jules go in his place. The cabin boy agreed to the deal and told Jules where to meet him the next morning.

Jules sneaked out of the house at dawn and made his

Jules (left) and his brother, Paul, (right) dreamed of traveling to far-off places.

way to a cafe on the docks. He carried a knapsack of food and some personal belongings, including his copybook. After money was exchanged, the cabin boy told Jules to go over to a table where some sailors were having coffee. Feeling both bold and hesitant, Jules introduced himself to them as the new cabin boy. The men put him in a rowboat and took him to the ship.

As the *Coralie* set sail, Jules stood on deck, fascinated by the activity around him. A thick, heavy chain was dragged along the deck as the anchor was dropped, and high over his head, men were balancing on the rigging and manning the huge, whipping sails. He was soon ordered to go below deck and get to work. He spent most of his time in the next few hours carrying food from the galley to the mess or to the captain's quarters, and carrying dirty dishes back to the galley where he had to wash them. He saw nothing of the Loire River or the coastline as they left Nantes far behind. Disappointed, he was still determined to have a grand adventure.

His grand adventure did not last long. He was allowed to go on deck at the first stop, the city of Paimboeuf, where he saw the same steamboat from Nantes puffing up the river. On its deck, his fist raised and expression furious, was Pierre Verne. The boy's old nurse, Mathurine, who lived close to the Vernes, had seen him sneaking out of the house. Paul had admitted that Jules had talked incessantly about the *Coralie* to him. Where Jules had disappeared to was easy for his parents to surmise.

Jules had mixed emotions when his father boarded the *Coralie*, seized him by the scruff of the neck, and dragged him back to Chantenay. His adventure had not lasted very long, but at least he had a story to tell and exciting memories that might last for years to come. He had gotten a small taste of shipboard life. On the other hand, working as a cabin boy was not much fun, so a small taste was all that he needed.

Sophie Verne had been nearly hysterical and was overjoyed to see her boy home safe. This did not prevent Pierre Verne from administering a severe spanking to his wandering son. Never again did Pierre want himself or his wife to go through such an ordeal. Although he was resentful of their interference, Jules made a promise to his parents. From now on he would travel to distant lands only "in my imagination." For the most part, it was a promise he would keep—in a way others of the Verne family could never have conceived.

Jules continued to write notes in his copybook. Soon the copious notes turned into stories. Mostly the primitive stories were imitations of things he had read, but they were also full of descriptions of things he imagined. He read and loved the many novels of Alexandre Dumas and Victor Hugo, as well as stories by foreign authors such as the American Edgar Allan Poe, who quickly became one of his all-time favorites. Poe's strange forays into grotesque and unexplored regions particularly excited young Jules.

In the evenings, Jules often accompanied his family to the Graslin Theater in Nantes, where he enjoyed many different dramatic works. He scribbled plots for his own plays in his copybook, hoping that one day he would actually see thespians enacting his stories on the stage. But all of his dreams were grounded by a hard reality: Whatever Jules might wish to become, his father wanted him to work in his law office. At sixteen, Jules began studying law.

The next few years for Jules consisted of toiling in his father's office by day, preparing for a career in law. At night he went to the theater, saw his friends, including his closest friends Edouard Bonamy and Aristide Hignard, and worked on his stories. He fell in love with his pretty cousin, Caroline Tronson, whom he had become close to around the time of the *Coralie* incident. Caroline lived in a boarding school in Nantes, and Jules used to visit her regularly. He found her to be a sympathetic soul. He kept his infatuation with her secret for years. By age nineteen, he was a rather handsome young man, tall and blond with an athletic build, and he decided to tell Caroline how he felt about her. She thought he was joking and laughed in his face.

Caroline may have hurt Jules's pride, but she did not break his spirit. He knew something was missing in his life. By all rights he should have been contented—he had a good job in his future, a loving family, good friends—but he felt restless and dissatisfied. He had promised to travel only in his imagination, but he still yearned to see other cities and have new experiences.

Then he received a letter from his friend Aristide Hignard, who had gone to Paris to study music. Hignard suggested that Jules come and stay with him. It was the only place for an artist to live, Aristide argued. There would be no running away this time; Jules went to his father and discussed it with him. His father promised him that if he applied himself diligently to his law studies, he would let him go to Paris in the springtime to take his first law exam.

This seemed like the perfect compromise. Jules was excited and happy, if a little impatient. He worked as hard as he could and counted the days until he could leave.

Chapter Two

Paris

In April 1847, Jules was finished with his law studies and ready to go to Paris. He traveled by steamboat to the city of Tours, and from there made the rest of the trip by railway. Fascinated by what he could see from the deck, and excited at being on a steamship, he stared at the shore for most of the journey from Nantes to Tours.

The hills leveled out to meadows as the topography flattened. The small islands in the middle of the river reminded him of Ile Feydeau. He saw ancient castles in the Loire Valley and wondered what kind of people lived in them in olden times. Everything he looked upon inspired his vivid imagination.

The steam engine of the train waiting for him in Tours was almost as fascinating to Jules as the steamboat. He had never been on a train, and as it chugged toward Paris, he hung out the window and watched the scenery—vineyards alternating with forests—speeding by. The train followed the familiar Loire River as it passed Orléans, the city freed by Joan of Arc during the Hundred Years War, and other, smaller cities. Finally, the train veered away at a sharp angle from the river and made its final approach into Paris.

Waiting for Jules on the platform in Paris was his great-aunt, Madame Charrüel—a white-haired, large, and very proper woman. After a warm greeting, she took him into her carriage, and they made off down the streets of Paris. Wide-eyed, Jules stared as Madame Charrüel tried hopelessly to make conversation. In a short while, the carriage pulled up to Madame Charrüel's house at Two Thérèse Street.

The following day, his great-aunt took her young charge on a tour of the city. He saw the Notre Dame Cathedral, which Victor Hugo's famous Hunchback had inhabited in one of Jules's favorite novels. Jules and his great-aunt walked along the beautiful Seine River, which divided the city into two distinct sections, or the Left and Right Banks. They took a tour of the Louvre Museum, which was full of magnificent art treasures, such as the *Mona Lisa* and the Rosetta Stone from ancient Egypt. Jules loved walking the streets of Paris and soaking in the atmosphere.

Still, he wished he were alone, or with his friend Aristide, instead of with his imposing great-aunt. He did manage to get together with Aristide a couple of times, but mostly he had to prepare for the exam, which (as far as his father was concerned) was his real reason for coming to Paris.

After Jules passed the exam, there was no more reason for him to stay in Paris. Reluctantly, but full of wonderful memories and a determination to return, he returned to Nantes.

Soon he was back in his father's office, trying to concentrate and get through the day while his mind was hundreds of miles away. While part of him wanted to quit the job and rush back to Paris, he knew it would be wiser to continue his work and studies. His father would then send him back to Paris for the second exam that he would need to take before becoming a lawyer.

In the evenings, Jules worked on his writing or attended meetings of a literary society that had formed in Nantes. Jules loved reading his work out loud to the group. The erudite members of this society were especially impressed by a play that he performed one night, reading all of the parts himself. He was encouraged by this group to concentrate on playwriting. He became even more determined to get back to Paris—not to study, or practice law—but to make a living as a playwright. This determination increased when his brother Paul left for the Antilles by boat, pursuing his dream of becoming a ship's captain. If his brother could pursue his dream, then he should be able to as well.

By the end of 1848, when Jules was twenty, it was time for him to return to Paris and take the next exam.

In his twenties, Verne decided to move to Paris and to pursue writing.

Jules managed to talk his father out of making him board with his great-aunt again. It was decided that he would go to Paris with his friend Edouard Bonamy. The two could take a room together. Both young men were excited by the prospect of this adventure.

There was some concern in the Verne and Bonamy families, however, because lately there had been riots in Paris. In 1848, most of Europe had been shaken by revolution. In France, King Louis-Philippe had been dethroned after a revolution and the Second Republic (the new regime) had been inaugurated. In a few years, this attempt at republican government with elected officials would come under the control of Louis Napolean, the nephew of the former emperor, but for now, the capital city seemed safe enough. Jules promised his parents that he would stay far away from any public demonstrations, although secretly he hoped to see something exciting. The Place de la Concorde, a famous square, was to be the site of many official ceremonies.

At Tours, the young men tried to board a troop train that would get them to Paris sooner, but they did not have the necessary papers to prove they were in the National Guard and were thrown off. Instead they caught the regular train and arrived at night in the middle of a snowstorm. Sheathed in white, the city seemed more beautiful than ever as the young men made their way from the train station to the Left Bank, on the south, or left-hand, side of the Seine. Jules knew that this was the

section of the city inhabited by bohemians and artists—writers, painters, and musicians of every stripe.

Walking through the snow-encrusted streets seeking
lodgings, they tried several boarding houses until they
found an inexpensive one on Rue de l'Ancienne
Comédie (Street of the Ancient Comedy). Jules and
Edouard were soon ensconced on the top floor of a
creaky old building. Then they located a cheap restau-
rant before looking up Aristide Hignard, who gave them
a lot of pointers on living inexpensively in Paris. Pierre
Verne had placed his son on a very tight allowance, as a
way to help keep Jules out of trouble in the notorious
City of Romance.

Jules could not even afford to go to the theater. The
only time he saw a play was when his Uncle
Châteaubourg, visiting Paris, took him to a performance
as a special treat. Aside from a roll for breakfast, Jules
could afford one meal a day. He and Edouard had only
one good suit between them, so should they both be
invited to a party that required formal attire, only one of
them could go. Luckily, their mothers sent them pack-
ages of food on a regular basis.

Uncle Châteaubourg introduced Jules to some of his
friends, but Jules found them all too political and rather
uncultured. He wanted to talk about books and authors,
not the pros and cons of the new regime. "Infernal
politics cast their drab mantle over the beauty of poetry," he wrote his parents. He was introduced, however,

to the editor of *Liberty* magazine, who told an awed Jules that he personally knew Victor Hugo and asked if Jules would be interested in meeting the famous author someday.

Jules was, of course, highly interested, and the editor took him to a party at Hugo's house, where the already-famous and soon-to-be-famous authors met. As there were many people around, Jules did not have much time to talk to Hugo, but he was thrilled nonetheless. Soon afterwards, he got to meet another famous novelist, Alexandre Dumas, and this meeting was much more propitious. Dumas held great "salons," or parties, where he entertained—and often fed—many artists and aspiring artists of uncertain means.

Dumas was the author of such books as *The Count of Monte Cristo* and *The Three Musketeers*, but before writing novels, he had been a playwright. He lived in a castle-like house called "Monte Cristo," which came complete with turbaned servants, high tower rooms, grounds with walkways and waterfalls—and many, many guests. Verne accompanied an acquaintance, a palm reader who was going to Monte Cristo to tell Dumas his fortune. When Dumas sat down next to him, Jules bombarded him with dozens of questions about his craft. Apparently, Dumas was flattered and took a liking to the enthusiastic young man.

From then on, Jules was a frequent guest in the writer's home. One evening he even sat in Dumas's private box at the theater during the opening night of a play based on *The Three Musketeers*. Edouard suggested that Jules go ahead and show Dumas some of his own plays—Dumas managed a theater in Paris—but Jules was afraid it would seem too pushy. After what he felt was a proper period of time, he brought Dumas three scripts and waited for his reaction.

Two of the short plays were historical dramas, which Dumas rejected, but after revising the third one slightly, he selected it for production at his Théâtre Historique. It was a one-act comedy called *Les Pailles rompues* (*Broken Straws*). The short play was about the "eternal triangle," two men in love with the same woman. Jules made no money from the play, but he did have the joy of watching from the wings as his piece was performed twelve times.

Broken Straws made Jules a small celebrity in a club for bachelors, *Onze sans Femmes (Eleven without Women),* which he had helped found with his friends. Better still, it raised his stock at home when the Graslin Theater in Nantes decided to do their own production of the play. On a trip home, Jules and his proud parents saw *Broken Straws* at the local theater. Sophie Verne was very pleased, but Pierre Verne found the play a bit too *risqué*. He worried that Jules might turn into one of these scandalous, controversial "Parisian writers," but Jules assured him that that would not be the case. He insisted that he was too devout a Roman Catholic to ever produce anything too shocking or sacrilegious.

Still, Jules did have news that upset his father. Writing, he declared, was not going to be just a sideline for him. Pierre Verne had expected his son to finish his studies in Paris, pass any further exams, and then return to Nantes to work with him in his office. Jules waited until he was back in Paris to write to his father and tell him that, except for visits, he would not be returning to Nantes, and he would not be entering the legal profession.

Jules insisted he had done his best and studied law diligently. He had even passed the second exam. But from now on, he told his father: "I am going to devote myself to literature. I may become a good writer, but I would never be anything but a poor lawyer." His father thought Jules was being foolish. The law would provide him with a steady income, something that was certainly not true of writing. A single success with a one-act play that brought him minor fame and no money was hardly enough to launch a career. But Jules's mind was made up, although he knew that his father would cut off his allowance and he would have to earn his own living. In a letter to his mother, he joked that she should make it her priority to find him a rich wife. Jules Verne had come to a crossroads in his life. So determined was he to succeed as a writer, so devoted was he to literature, that he could settle for nothing less. It may have been that his father was right and he had an unrealistic view of the possibility of his success. Although, unlike other young writers of his day, he had established contacts with professional writers who were able to help him, he knew that there might be very tough times ahead. He was willing to take the chance to pursue his dream.

Verne's first published story appeared in *Musée des Familles.*

He tightened his belt and worked on more plays, short stories, and articles. *The Fate of Jean Morénas* dealt with a mysterious man who contrives to free the wrongly imprisoned title character from a dockyard manned by convicts. He never sold it. Some stories he managed to get published in a magazine called *Musée des Familles (Family Museum)*. *A Drama in the Air* (1851) tells of two men who go up in a balloon. When one of them determines to commit suicide, the other tries to prevent his jumping from the gondola, and a terrible struggle ensues. Right away, Jules showed his propensity for unusual, highly-charged dramatic situations.

Musée des Familles took many of Jules's stories after *A Drama in the Air*, which was successful. *A Drama in Mexico* (1851), about a mutiny in the Spanish Navy, was purported to be "historical fact" but was really fiction. *Martin Paz* (1852) concerned natives in Peru suffering under Spanish oppression. *Master Zacharius* (1854) tells of a sixteenth century clockmaker who becomes ensnared by a terrible demon who looks like a kind of "human clock." This and other stories showed the strong influence of Edgar Allen Poe, who was at this time more famous in France than his native land.

It was Alexandre Dumas who encouraged Verne to incorporate scientific elements into his stories. Other writers had their own specialties, and he wanted to carve out his own niche and write scientific stories the way Dumas wrote historical stories. He knew of no one else who published stories incorporating scientific fact or stories that combined speculation with scientific ideas. It was for that reason that he wrote *A Drama in the Air*—real-life balloonists were making headlines every day. Eventually, balloonists would play a part in his first full-length work of fiction and his first bestseller.

Chapter Three

Struggling

Jules discovered that it was impossible to survive on the income he made from selling the occasional story. He began to wonder if his father had been right. His friendship with the great Alexandre Dumas and the mounting of *Broken Straws* had given him a false sense of security. Life as a struggling writer turned out to be a lot tougher than he had expected. He was beginning to despair when an opportunity came along that provided some needed relief.

He learned of an opening for a secretarial position at the Théâtre Lyrique (Lyric Theater). Jules would write and mail announcements of the upcoming plays, see that the proper posters were put up in front of the theater and around Paris, and perform other clerical duties. The salary was not great, but it was enough to pay his rent and feed him, with a little left over. Dumas gave him a recommendation and Jules was hired.

Working in a theater encouraged Jules to write plays. He hoped he would have greater success as a playwright than as a short story writer. But his duties and his long hours at the theater left him too tired to concentrate on his work once he got home. He would sit in his little room and try to keep his eyes open as the pen drooped in his hand.

In his early twenties, Jules felt as if life—and success—were passing him by. The bohemian life style that he had thought would be so exciting had become stark. He was not starving, as other artists were, due to his job at the theater, but month followed month with no improvement.

Jules began to develop ailments. He developed bad headaches from writing by candlelight at all hours, and tossed and turned in bed all night, unable to sleep. The constant worrying about his future gave him stomachaches. Eventually he developed a facial paralysis that affected the left side of his face. He could barely open his eye on that side, and his mouth was slightly contorted. Friends advised him that he needed a vacation, and he spent some time with relatives in Dunkirk on the North Sea.

Refreshed by his vacation and feeling much better about his prospects, Jules returned to Paris and worked harder than ever. The theater put on some of his plays, usually farces, and he sold more stories to Parisian magazines. He began to feel that his secretarial duties were preventing him from writing. After saving what he hoped was a sufficient sum, he quit his job in November 1855 and decided to write full-time.

That summer, Jules traveled to the city of Amiens, north of Paris on the Somme River, to attend a friend's wedding. While everyone else's eyes were on the bride, Jules could not take his eyes off the bride's pretty sister. Her name was Honorine Morel, and she was a young widow with two daughters, Suzanne and Valentine. Jules contrived to ride in the same carriage as Honorine as they went from the church to the reception, and the two got to know each other better.

At age twenty-eight, Jules was so smitten that he was determined to become a suitable husband. He could not afford to take care of a wife and two children on his current writer's income. He decided to take another "normal" job despite his feelings about the last one. Only this time, he would have to make enough money to care for an entire family. He asked his father if he would buy him a share in a stockbroker's business and had to explain why. Pierre and Sophie were stunned to learn that their "bohemian" son was now about to marry a widow with two children. Nevertheless, Pierre agreed to loan him the money he needed.

Having come to accept how much writing meant to his son, Pierre was concerned that Jules seemed so willing to throw it all away after working hard at his writing for many years. Jules assured his father that he

Jules married Honorine Morel, a young widow with two daughters, in 1857.

had not given up on his dream. He planned to work half a day on the stock exchange and spend the rest of the time crafting plays and stories. Pierre wondered if Jules would be able to make much money at his new profession if he worked only half a day. "What I need is to be happy," Jules wrote him, "neither more nor less."

Jules's father was also unimpressed with the actual wedding ceremony and traditional breakfast that took place on January 10, 1857. The whole affair seemed slipshod. He worried about how his son and daughter-in-law and her two young girls would get along in Jules's cramped apartment. The only thing that comforted Pierre was the knowledge that Honorine, who seemed levelheaded as compared to Jules, would keep his son firmly grounded.

Two years went by, and Jules and his ready-built family were still living in the small apartment. The only relief they got were frequent trips to Amiens to see Jules's understanding in-laws. In Paris, Jules would rise at five and try to get in some writing time before he had to go to the stock market at ten. Honorine would do her best to keep her daughters quiet so that their stepfather could work.

Jules did not enjoy his work as a stockbroker. In fact, he hated the workaday business world with its dull jobs and conventional outlook. Colleagues on the stock exchange remarked that he was "better at banter than at business." He sought out like-minded souls on the floor of the stock exchange and became friends with a few of the more cultured and well read among them.

One afternoon, Jules received a visit from his old friend Aristide Hignard, who was having no more luck with his music than Jules was with his stories. Aristide's brother worked for a shipping line, and he could get them free passage on a ship bound for Scotland. Aristide suggested that Jules's brother, Paul, who was currently back in Nantes, join them. Honorine was very understanding as Jules explained to her that this was his first and perhaps only chance to actually go to sea as he had always dreamed.

Honorine was a perfect wife for Jules. She knew how dissatisfied he was with his life and his work on the stock exchange, and she agreed that he should take this vacation while she minded her daughters. They would go visit her relatives in Amiens while he was gone. Jules was overjoyed at her reaction.

The boat left from the pier at Nantes. As always,

Jules jotted down his impressions in a notebook. They sailed to the British Isles and made port at Liverpool in England. From there they made their way to Edinburgh, the capital of Scotland. Jules remembered all the stories he had loved by Sir Walter Scott that took place in that country and could hardly believe that he was actually there. The young man was impressed by the beauty of Scotland, its castles and meadows and lakes, but one particular feature stood out in his memory: the forbidding, dark coal mines and abandoned pits with their rusted, discarded machinery.

On the way back to France, the boat docked at London, where Verne saw hundreds of workers assembling a steamship named the *Great Eastern*. This huge ship was built to sail across the ocean. Jules wrote a fanciful story—part fact and part fiction—about his journey to Scotland that was never published.

The following year, Jules went on a cargo boat to Norway for several weeks. Trekking to the fjords through snow and cold winds, he got a slight but imagination-stirring taste of "Arctic life" and "heroic exploration." He kept busy in quieter moments jotting down more half-formed ideas for future stories.

Jules wrote a great deal during this period, but published little. He was full of ideas but uncertain which of them would bring him the greatest success. He did have some luck as a playwright. He collaborated on the libretto of an operetta, *The Inn in the Ardennes* (1859), and wrote the book for a musical comedy, *Monsieur de Chimpanzé* (1860), in which an ape dressed up like a man enters polite society and winds up making monkeys of the pretentious humans he meets. Aristide Hignard provided the music for these plays. The following year, Jules came out with his first three-act play, a marital comedy called *Eleven Days' Siege* that was briefly performed at the Vaudeville Theatre.

At home, there was one production of which Jules was extremely proud. On August 3, 1861, Honorine presented her husband with her third—and his first, and only, child—their son Michel. Soon after, however, Jules's joy turned into depression. He now had *five* people living in the small quarters. After four years of marriage, he still could not afford a larger place. The new baby's crying at all hours disturbed his writing.

To find some peace and quiet, as well as stimulating conversation, Jules joined a literary group called *Le Cercle de la Press Scientifique*. It was here that Jules met a man who was to have a great impact on his future. Félix Tournachon was a successful photographer who used the professional name of "Nadar." Tournachon had already acheived fame as the man who had taken the very first aerial photograph—of the rooftops of Paris. Nadar wanted to build a flying machine, but he needed money. To raise funds, he intended to build a hundred-foot balloon called *Le Géant* (The Giant) that would have a thirteen-foot gondola. From this gondola, he would take many more aerial photographs that he would sell.

Jules was intrigued by Nadar, and wrote about him for the *Musée des Familles*. The subject seemed too big and important for just one magazine article. He decided to write about balloonists, especially those who used balloons for exploration. Certain that he had finally hit upon a winning formula, Verne steeled himself to write a full-length, non-fiction manuscript on the subject of balloonists.

Verne's work began with a history of real-life balloonists, including Nadar, before he speculated on the many ways in which balloons could be used in the future. He was encouraged by the fact that so many Frenchmen had been pioneers in ballooning. The first man to go up in a balloon was Jean de Rozier of France. The resulting book was, as many of his later books would be, a combination of fact and educated fancy.

Unfortunately, none of the publishers Jules submitted the manuscript to shared his enthusiasm for the subject. Ballooning was still seen as a rather silly, useless pastime, a perception that Jules had hoped to eradicate with his book. All he got for his hard work was a long series of rejection slips. He expressed his bitterness in a short story entitled "The Humbug" (1863), which made fun of entrepreneurs without talent or scruples who managed to get ahead while those with genuine aptitude got nowhere.

Félix Tournachon, who went by the name "Nadar," influenced Verne in his writing about ballooning. Nadar would fly his balloon, *Le Géant* (The Giant), three times before crashing it in Germany.

Pierre-Jules Hetzel agreed to publish Verne's *Five Weeks in a Balloon. (Courtesy of Bibliothèque Nationale, France.)*

After the manuscript received its fifteenth rejection, Jules took it out of its envelope and threw it into the fireplace. Dismayed, Honorine reached into the fire and quickly pulled it out before it burned. She chided her husband for his defeatist attitude and reminded him that there were still other publishers in Paris. Bolstered by his wife's confidence in his ability, Jules decided to try at least one more publishing house before consigning the manuscript to the ashes.

It was providence that he did. The very next publishing house, Hetzel, was named after its owner Pierre-Jules Hetzel, who under the name of P.J. Stahl also wrote children's stories. Jules took the manuscript directly to the publisher's headquarters on Eighteen Rue Jacob. Hetzel lived in an apartment above his offices and an associate sent Jules up to see him. Hetzel was having coffee in bed when Jules arrived. He took the manuscript from him and told him to return in a couple of weeks for his opinion.

The second time Jules met Hetzel, the publisher was

again in his bed. He told the anxious writer that he had read and enjoyed his manuscript, but he could not see himself publishing it unless some changes were made.

At first, Jules felt like running out of the room in anger. He was tired of the almost constant rejection. But he remained calm and listened to what Hetzel had to say. The publisher told him that although the book had many fascinating points of interest, it lacked a strong narrative structure. Part of it was fact, followed by speculation, then more fact, then fantasy, and so on. Why not rewrite the book as fact-based fiction?

A large section of Verne's book dealt with the possibility of exploring Africa by balloon. Hertzel suggested that Verne expand that section into a novel. Instead of real-life balloonists throughout history, the protagonists could be characters partially modeled on those heroes. The rest could be filled in by Verne's imagination.

Excited by the possibilities, Jules shook hands with Hetzel and promised to return with a new manuscript as soon as he was able.

Chapter Four

Ballooning

As Jules worked on the rewrite of his balloonist book, he thought back to a conversation he had had with Alexandre Dumas, who had built a successful career by writing historical fiction. Verne told Dumas that he wanted to write science-based fiction in the hope that it would become his specialty. He knew of no other person who wrote science-based fiction consistently. Jules had allowed himself to be sidetracked from his goal. Now he was convinced that the publisher Hetzel had put him back on the right path. Working at a white heat and using all of the research and some of the incidents in his manuscript, he fashioned a fictional adventure story that he entitled *Five Weeks in a Balloon* (1863). He finished the new book-length manuscript in only two weeks.

Hetzel was very pleased with the new book, suggested a few minor revisions that Jules had no problem implementing, and offered Verne a contract. *Five Weeks in a Balloon* was published a few weeks later and was an immediate success—a bestseller, in fact. Sales were helped because the exploits of real-life balloonists, including Nadar, were constantly featured in newspaper stories. But Verne's story was also considered a "ripping good adventure yarn" by critics and the reading public.

The story of *Five Weeks in a Balloon* deals with three men—Doctor Samuel Fergusson of the Royal Geographical Society, his manservant Joe, and a Scotsman named Dick Kennedy—who cross Africa in a balloon and have a number of exciting adventures. Although aware of the explorers who failed to return from many of the previous trips to Africa, the single-minded Fergusson will not be deterred from his goal of exploring the unknown continent. He believes a balloon will help his party safely get to places others have failed to reach. Fergusson is the first in a series of uncompromising Verne characters who would take any risk to achieve their aims regardless of the danger to themselves or to their companions.

Fergusson and company actually employ two balloons on the trip, a smaller one inside the outer one. This arrangement comes in handy when the outer balloon is destroyed. An apparatus is used to heat and expand hydrogen gas that inflates the balloon and keeps it in the air at the proper altitude. A car, or gondola, consisting of hempen cord with an iron covering and elastic springs, carries the trio from place to place. This vehicle is christened *Victoria*. Verne incorporated all of the latest information on balloons and imagined a workable variation based on what was known. This act of using scientific knowledge as a springboard for the writer's imagination is the core of science fiction. The air ship *Victoria* could go places and do things that no real balloon could at the time.

The first port of call is Zanzibar, where the trio set up their balloon and prepare to depart. The natives are outraged by the idea of the proposed journey. They think the balloon is meant to travel all the way to the sun or the moon. Because they worship these heavenly bodies, such a journey would be a sacrilege. Fergusson and company manage to take off before the natives can stop them, but the next few days are full of harrowing exploits.

They are attacked by apes that climb up through the tree branches to get at the balloon. Then they are dragged by an elephant whose trunk wraps around the car's anchor and nearly dashes them to the ground. They encounter man-eating lions at a well within an oasis; and witness a miles-wide cloud of locusts strip all vegetation from the ground in a matter of minutes. Attacked by condors while three thousand feet in the air, the outer balloon is rent by their beaks and claws and the explorers begin to fall toward a lake below. The book's most bizarre wildlife episode features a flock of "incendiary pigeons" that are set upon the *Victoria* by an angry governor in the town of Loggoum. Fiery squibs are affixed to the tails of the birds, but the *Victoria* manages to evade them.

In addition to dangerous animals, there are superstitious, murderous natives and even cannibals. A gro-

Verne's first published book, *Five Weeks in a Balloon,* became a bestseller.

tesque segment deals with a "tree of human heads," a giant sycamore tree adorned with severed heads affixed to the branches with daggers. Human bones surround the tree. Verne somewhat glosses over a gruesome scene of battle carnage when two tribes hack at each other, their women fighting amongst themselves for the trophies of decapitated craniums. A tribal chief slices off an opponent's arm and begins to gnaw on it. Appalled, the Scotsman takes aim from *Victoria* and kills the cannibal with one shot.

In spite of all this misadventure, Verne still had a

great deal to learn about how to structure and sustain suspense over a book-length manuscript. The action sometimes plods from one episode to the next, sometimes descriptions are vague and the characterizations are thin. For instance, Joe, the manservant, seems little more than a human version of a brave fox terrier with few distinguishing characteristics.

Today, Verne's attitude toward Africans and Arabs would be considered blatantly racist. However, his racial attitude reflected the general assumptions made by most nineteenth century Western Europeans. Much of the behavior and habits of the tribes he used in the novel was taken from descriptions made by writers who had traveled the continent.

Hetzel was very pleased by the success of *Five Weeks in a Balloon*, and he offered Verne a life-long contract. He wanted to start a new magazine entitled *Le Magazine d'Education et de Recreation (The Journal of Education and Recreation)*. Subsequent books by Verne would first be serialized in the magazine, then bound together between hard covers. Hetzel asked Jules if he thought he could come up with two new novels a year. Jules accepted enthusiastically after Hetzel agreed to pay him twenty thousand francs per year.

Jules's success in his chosen career caused him to make two major changes in his life. First, he quit his job at the stock exchange. "Boys, I'm leaving you," he told his co-workers. "I've had an idea. If it succeeds I shall have come across a gold mine and go on ceaselessly writing." Second, he moved Honorine and the children into a house in Boulogne Woods, a suburb of Paris. It was a larger house where they could entertain, the children could play in the yard, and Jules could have a study where he could research and write in privacy.

Jules's friend Nadar finally got his balloon, *Le Géant*, off the ground. It had two successful, if brief, flights that same year. On its third flight in Germany, the balloon crashed to the ground, but luckily neither Nadar, nor his wife, who had accompanied him on the flight, were badly injured.

Once settled in his new home, Jules pondered what the topic of his next novel should be. Hetzel, of course, wanted something similar to *Five Weeks in a Balloon*. But Jules had something else in mind, a short tragic novel entitled *Paris in the Twentieth Century*.

Although *Paris in the Twentieth Century* was completed the same year that *Five Weeks in a Balloon* was published, it is very likely that most of it was written even earlier. *Paris in the Twentieth Century* was clearly written by a struggling writer full of pessimism for his future—and the future in general—not by the newly successful novelist.

The novel concerns a sixteen-year-old boy named Michel Dufrénoy, named after Verne's son, who is a misfit orphan in a future Parisian culture that derides art and cares only for technology. His relatives are embarrassed that Michel has won a prize for some Latin verses he composed. Michel is sent to work in a bank, which he hates, then tries to make a living as a writer. He has a good friend, Quinsonnas, who is a composer (modeled on Aristide Hignard) and dearly loves his Uncle Huguenin (modeled on Francis de Châteaubourg), who loves books as much as he does.

Huguenin works in the library's classic fiction department but has little to do as no one reads the great masters any longer. He also has a huge private library at home that Michel marvels at. Michel gains consolation from his uncle and the very few like-minded friends that he meets, and falls in love with a girl, Lucy, whom he cannot afford to marry. Michel tries one unsuitable job after another, becomes a hack writer churning out disposable plays, then quits in disgust. Making the rounds of publishers, he is unable to find one of them to read the volume of poetry he had had such hopes for.

Michel spends the last of his money on a flower for Lucy, only to learn that she and her grandfather have moved and he cannot find them. Unable to survive in a cold world that devalues culture and the artist, Michel winds up dying of exposure and hunger in a cemetery as he wanders from the tomb of one great French writer to another.

In *Paris in the Twentieth Century,* Verne shows amazing prescience. He describes everything from fax machines to mammoth chain bookstores. The book may have been fueled by fear and bitterness, but these otherwise acrid emotions helped Verne create one of his most interesting and memorable works of fiction. It is full of his youthful contempt for a love of money and material gain over culture, learning, and a true appreciation of human artistic endeavor.

Paris in the Twentieth Century is the one book that Verne put his life experiences, attitudes, and frustrations into. Although the hero Michel has been

Verne named the protagonist of *Paris in the Twentieth Century* after his son, Michel, pictured here at ten years old. *(Courtesy of Bibliothèque Municipale, Nantes, France.)*

described as "a fool . . . and a ninny" for ignoring the reality of his situation, he was clearly Verne's stand-in. The citizens of Nantes thought that Jules was foolish for dropping the steady employment of law to dedicate himself to the risky career of literature. In Michel's futuristic world, the odds of success for a writer are even worse than they were in Jules's day.

Jules wanted to be considered a serious writer, not just a producer of adventure stories. He wanted to publish something that would shake up and galvanize modern society. It is ironic that one of this great science-fiction writer's best books decried the emphasis of science over art. But Hetzel only wanted to give the public what they expected from Jules Verne. He rejected *Paris in the Twentieth Century* unceremoniously, dismissing it as "petty journalism." Hetzel may also have been annoyed at the way Jules tweaked him in his story when, in referring to French writers of the "long-ago" nineteenth century, he mentions Stahl (Hetzel's pen name), "so scrupulously published by the house of Hetzel." Hetzel was a bit sensitive that he published his own work under a pseudonym and may have thought that Jules was laughing at him. In any case, Hetzel was unable to see what a visionary Jules Verne really was. He only knew that *Paris in the Twentieth Century* was not the kind of work the two men had talked about when he offered Jules a lifetime contract. Jules put the manuscript of *Paris in the Twentieth Century* away. It was not discovered again until many years after his death.

Just as the real-life exploration of Africa had informed Verne's *Five Weeks in a Balloon,* the recent investigation of the frozen lands of the Arctic compelled him to write another book.

In the papers, he read about Sir John Franklin's disappearance on an expedition to the Arctic Circle and his wife's efforts to rescue him. The U.S. Navy had attempted to find a passage to the North Pole through

Greenland. With these events in mind, Jules began putting together notes for a story of an expedition to the Arctic Circle.

Jules was also intrigued by the idea of people descending into tunnels and caverns inside the earth and exploring whatever inner world might exist there. He had done a great deal of research into spelunkers, people who explored the vast caves near the surface, but what if they were able to descend much, much deeper, he wondered.

The two ideas—traveling to the North Pole and exploring the inside of Earth—were both appealing and revolved in his mind with equal fascination. It was the second idea that took root first, however, and *A Journey to the Center of the Earth* (1864) became his next project.

Chapter Five

Remarkable Journeys

Jules Verne was not the first author to use the idea of a hollow, inhabited Earth in his fiction. He may have read about it in an obscure eighteenth century novel by Baron Ludvig Holberg. The difference is that Verne's fantastic tale had a basis in what was then up-to-date science. He interviewed French seismologist Charles Sainte-Claire Deville to gather information to build a solid, scientific foundation to support the story's more imaginative elements. The geological descriptions and technical equipment employed in the novel are based on what was known in 1864.

In *A Journey to the Center of the Earth* a German professor, Otto Lidenbrock, finds a coded message on parchment hidden inside an old book. Ever since Jules had read Poe's story, "The Goldbug," he had been fascinated by cryptography. Lidenbrock's nephew, Axel, finally works out that the words have been written backwards. Arne Saknussemm, a sixteenth century alchemist, who claims that he actually reached the center of the earth and managed to return safely to the surface, had signed the message. (Verne may have based Saknussemm on an Icelandic scholar of the seventeenth century named Arni Magnusson.)

To Axel's dismay, Lidenbrock decides that he and Axel will follow in the alchemist's footsteps. As they prepare to descend into an extinct volcano for the first leg of their journey, a stoic Icelandic guide named Hans joins them. Hans will follow them anywhere as long as he is faithfully paid.

Thus begins one of Verne's finest adventure stories. His storytelling skills had improved since his first book, and *Journey* is consistently absorbing, intense, and harrowing. At one point Axel is separated from the others miles beneath the earth and finds himself without light or water. Verne keeps piling on one incident after the next, and his ability to create new perils never fails him.

Jules chose to dismiss theories that the center of the earth would be unbearably hot. Because it was less likely any real explorers would follow in the path of Lidenbrock and company (as they might his balloonists), he was freer to create his own incredible world inside the planet. At that time, there was a lot of talk about the prehistoric animals that had once inhabited Earth. European paleontologists, such as Mary Anning, were uncovering fossils, and debate was growing over how and when life had begun. Verne had his explorers come upon an underground "central sea" full of living, breathing, prehistoric saurians. Electrified clouds that function as a kind of enormous aurora borealis light up the gigantic cavern that holds the sea. The book's most thrilling chapter concerns the disaster that nearly occurs when the trio's small raft is almost swamped by the raging battle between a crocodile-like *Ichthyosaurus* and a long-necked *Plesiosaurus*.

Over a hundred years before *Jurassic Park* (and several decades before Sir Arthur Conan Doyle's *The Lost World*) Verne introduced modern readers to prehistoric monsters in a work of fiction. When nineteenth century scientists concluded that some kind of human being existed in prehistory (although not concurrent with dinosaurs), Verne added chapters in which Lidenbrock and his nephew spot a twelve foot "antediluvian shepherd" tending to a herd of mastodons! Axel also dreams of an ape almost the size of King Kong.

At the novel's climax, the three explorers ascend to the surface much faster than they descended by riding on top of a wave of boiling water that is being pushed to the surface by lava rising from another erupting volcano. Verne undoubtedly supposed that if his readers believed his heroes could encounter dinosaurs beneath the surface, they would also accept that they could survive being blown out of an active volcano.

The characters of Verne's *A Journey to the Center of the Earth* sail on a subterranean sea in a battered raft.

A Journey to the Center of the Earth (1864) was a greater success than *Five Weeks in a Balloon*. Even today the story stirs the imagination, despite our increased knowledge of the inside of our planet. In 1998, a French scientist named Yves Cansi and an American seismologist at Northwestern University named Emile Okal proved that "inside a liquid core, the center of the earth is actually a giant ball of solid iron."

Verne's next book was inspired by an Edgar Allan Poe short story he had enjoyed in which a trip to the moon (by balloon, no less) turns out to be a hoax. *From the Earth to the Moon* (1865) is a light-hearted but "accurate" look at a trip to the moon via a cylinder shot out of an enormous gun. The story, set after the U.S. Civil War, features the bored members of an American gun club who figure out a way for a human to reach the moon. Verne praises American ingenuity and resolve, even as he spoofs what he sees as violent, dramatic, and dangerously stubborn tendencies.

The members of the gun club plan to anchor a huge cannon to the ground and fire a projectile with explosives. The projectile, which will reach the moon if it is discharged when the satellite is in its closest orbit to the earth, is an aluminum shell twelve inches thick and weighing 19,250 pounds. Twelve hundred furnaces going at once are employed to melt the sixty thousand tons of cast-iron required to form the nine-hundred-foot cannon.

No one considers putting anyone into this cylinder until the club receives a message from a Frenchman, one Michel Ardan, (whose name is an anagram for his friend Nadar,) who is traveling to Florida where the projectile is to be launched. He wants to be the first man on the moon, and no sensible objections will put him off. When asked how he intends to get back to earth, he simply says, "I am not coming back!" It is decided that two members of the gun club will travel with the Frenchman. There is some fear that all of Florida will explode when the gargantuan cannon is fired.

The three men never do reach their destination, however. Instead, it is suggested that the projectile has become fixed in orbit around our moon and will become in turn the moon's satellite for the rest of time.

Verne's fans naturally enough wanted to know what had happened to Ardan and the others, so Verne wrote a sequel entitled *Around the Moon* (1870) in which the projectile has become the moon's satellite because of a collision with a small asteroid.

The author had to keep his imagination from running amok—no monsters on the moon—for by the 1860s, astronomers had mapped the various lunar mountains and "seas" and knew a great deal about its composition and atmosphere. No one had ever mapped or looked at the center of the earth through a telescope, but the moon was a different story. Verne believed that the moon may have once been habitable, but was no longer.

Today we know that Verne's idea of shooting a projectile from a giant cannon would never have worked. The projectile and its inhabitants would have been destroyed in an instant. Verne was on the mark in suggesting that water could be used as a shock absorber, although it would not have helped in the case of such massive acceleration. Verne was also prescient in suggesting that rockets attached to the projectile could be used to guide the spacecraft and to slow its descent.

The gun club characters also appear in a third book, *Topsy Turvey* (1889), when they attempt to shift the planet off its axis for what they hope will be beneficial results, such as making polar exploration more practical and stabilizing the climate.

Jules received strange fan mail because of his moon books. Some people wrote and asked him if they could go to the moon with him on his next trip. Women offered to give birth to the first child born on the moon if Jules Verne would agree to be the father. "Play Adam to some daughter of Eve up there?" he bellowed. "No, thank you!" Honorine threw these letters into the fireplace.

Jules's book on the Arctic Circle, *The Adventures of Captain Hatteras*, came out in 1866. Although this story was much less fantastic than the previous ones, it was no less intense or entertaining. An unknown person hires a group of sailors to go on a long voyage on a newly built ship called the *Forward*. Verne creates sus-

In Verne's *Around the Moon,* the astronauts splashdown in the Pacific Ocean within three miles of the site where the *Apollo 9* astronauts would land one hundred years later.

pense by withholding both the identity of the captain, who at first communicates only with notes, and the ship's destination. When a grumpy dog appears with another note in its mouth, some of the crew think the demonic canine is the captain.

It turns out that Captain Hatteras has been on board all the time, disguised as one of the sailors. A wealthy Englishman, who was the sole survivor of his last voyage to the North Pole, Hatteras knew he would have trouble forming a crew under his real name. Just as Lidenbrock wanted to get to the earth's center, Michel Ardan to the moon, and Fergusson to fly over Africa, Hatteras is determined to make sure the English advance farther into the Arctic Circle than the Americans.

There are great difficulties awaiting him and the crew, however. The *Forward* is trapped on all sides by icebergs and nearly crushed. When the ship hits land and can go no farther, the coal begins to run out and the temperature drops to sixty-six degrees below zero. Hatteras and some others decide to travel three hundred miles over the ice to get to a cache of coal that was left by a previous expedition. Fighting the extreme cold all of the way, they also run into hungry bears and wolves and have to deal with storms and fog. In one sequence, they rescue an American captain from under the frozen bodies of his comrades. When they return to their ship, they find the angry sailors have set it on fire and fled with the provisions.

Against all odds, Hatteras decides to continue on to the North Pole. After many more tribulations, Hatteras is the first to reach the destination. Sailing a sloop across the water to the North Pole, he climbs to the top of a volcano—and goes mad.

Verne's descriptions of sailors lost in the snow, struggling against the effects of frigid temperatures, are highly suspenseful. The book was another best-selling triumph for Jules.

With four big hits in a row, Jules Verne should have been the happiest man in the world. But he was to discover there was a downside to celebrity.

Chapter Six

Celebrity

By his late thirties, Jules Verne was a famous, and wealthy, man. He also felt the pressure of having to create new stories that topped his previous ones. He and his family now enjoyed a comfortable standard of living that depended on him selling large numbers of books. He had waited so long for the kind of life that he and his family now enjoyed, but the stress was not over. Earlier he had worried about attaining success. Now he worried that it might slip away.

Under this economic pressure, Jules knew only one thing to do: work, work, and work some more. He took long walks, brooding about plots and how to develop them. He researched for hours. "I start by making a draft of a new story. I never begin without knowing what the beginning, middle, and end will be," he told an interviewer. He first did a rough draft in pencil, leaving enough room in the margin for copious notes and additions. Then he would write a second draft in ink.

He continued to make revisions and corrections even after he received the first set of proofs, or galleys, from the publisher. "I do not seem to have a grip of my subject until I see my work in print. I not only correct something in every sentence but I rewrite whole chapters. I [do] as many as ten revisions." Verne would occasionally make changes in a story between the time it was serialized in a magazine and released as a hardcover book.

To produce two long, complicated, heavily researched and revised books a year, not to mention mull over many future projects, Jules had little time to do anything but work. This busy schedule began to take its toll. Old health problems came back to plague him: insomnia, headaches, and stomach troubles. He also suffered from severe muscle cramps in his arm. When he was afflicted with facial paralysis again, his wife insisted he get away for a while.

Jules rejected Honorine's suggestion to go home to see his parents. All four of his siblings were now married with children, and his parents' house was always full of people. Many of his neighbors, and even people he did not know, wanted to come over to talk to the now-famous Jules Verne. That would hardly help him to relax, as Jules had a horror of meeting the public, no matter how admiring they might be. He was often rude to strangers who approached him and rarely used his status to arrange meetings with other famous people. It

By his thirties, Verne had acheived the kind of success he had dreamed of as a young man. *(Courtesy of Bibliothèque Municipale, Nantes, France.)*

may be that he was shy, as are many writers, or hated to have his thoughts interrupted.

He decided to rent a house in the tiny fishing village of Le Crotoy, where he could be near the sea and his beloved boats. Honorine went along with it, but was dismayed that the village was so isolated. Her daughters were even more disappointed to leave Paris and their friends. But their son, Michel, was overjoyed to be living on the water. Jules bought a shrimp boat from one of the locals and adapted it for his own uses. He christened it the *Saint Michel* after his son, hired two fishermen as crew, and made himself the captain.

He was a "Sunday sailor" with no interest in shrimping or fishing, and he left the more difficult work to the two crewmen. But the fresh sea air served as a tonic to renew his spirits and to give him a calmer, happier outlook on life. Honorine was annoyed that she hardly saw her husband, who was always out on the boat when he was not working. "Hardly here and he's gone again. He simply can't stay still," she complained.

Before long his health was restored, and he grew the fulsome beard that became his trademark. Some thought he grew the beard to avoid using a straight razor on his face while sailing, others because it made him look more like a sea captain. It was more probable Jules was afraid his facial paralysis would return. He was sensitive about his looks as he grew older.

Jules felt well enough not only to write a new novel, but also take on a non-fiction project, *An Illustrated Geography of France* (1867), to finish for Hetzel after the original author died before it was completed. His new novel, *The Children of Captain Grant* (1867), was an adventure story. Also influenced by Poe, it hinges on an incomplete message found in a bottle. The message is from the title character, who has been set adrift with two crew members and is asking for rescue. Grant's two children, a geographer named Paganel, and a Scotsman named Laird, head off on a yacht to find the men. The foursome travel to South America and have many grand adventures before realizing they are searching for Grant in the wrong part of the world. Next they sail to Australia, where they face further peril before rescuing the captain and his crew. It was the longest novel Verne had written up to that date.

The Children of Captain Grant sold well, but Verne's next novel became one of his most famous. The idea for *Twenty Thousand Leagues under the Sea* (1870) came to him while he was on a vacation after finishing *The Children of Captain Grant* and the nonfiction work. He had remembered seeing the *Great Eastern* steamship being built years before. Since that time, *Great Eastern* had laid a transatlantic cable on the ocean floor. American President Andrew Johnson had sent the first message over the cable to England's Queen Victoria. For the vacation, Jules and his brother Paul decided to sail on the *Great Eastern* from Liverpool to New York and back.

This trip provided Jules with material for *Twenty Thousand Leagues* as well as other projects. He interviewed sailors and the captain on the ship, visited Niagara Falls in New York State near the Canadian border, and collected enough information for several novels. *A Floating City* (1871) wove a fictional storyline into his account of the Atlantic voyage. He used Niagara Falls as a climactic setting for one of his historical novels, *A Family without a Name* (1889). But most importantly, he incorporated all that he saw and learned into a manuscript with the working title of *Voyage beneath the Oceans* that became *Twenty Thousand Leagues under the Sea*.

At the start of the novel, a ship sets sail to locate the unknown marine animal that has been spotted by several ships—and caused damage to one of them. On board are Pierre Aronnax, a professor in the Paris Museum; his devoted manservant, Conseil; and Ned Land, a world-famous Canadian harpooner. The "animal" turns out to be a submarine like none the world has never seen before. The *Nautilus* runs on electricity—decades before it was employed in the real world. (Edison perfected the light bulb about ten years after publication of *Twenty Thousand Leagues*.) Aronnax, Conseil, and Land are captured by the sub's master, the mysterious Captain Nemo, who takes them on an undersea voyage "twenty thousand leagues" long.

A trip to the sunken city of Atlantis is a highlight of the novel. In another chapter, they journey inside the extinct volcano that supplies Nemo his raw materials. The *Nautilus*'s plight when it is trapped under an ice flow and the air supply is running out provides some of the most exciting scenes.

Captain Nemo is one of Verne's most fascinating, if enigmatic, creations. Originally, Jules had wanted Nemo to be a Polish man who hated Russians because of Russian oppression of Poland. Publisher Hetzel, however, was afraid the Russians would ban Verne's books, which sold well there. He suggested making Nemo an opponent of slavery who fires on slave ships. Jules decided to leave the whole thing a big mystery—until he wrote the sequel.

Contrary to popular opinion, Verne did not invent the submarine. In fact, his fictional *Nautilus* is named after a sub built by Robert Fulton twenty-seven years earlier. Unlike Verne's huge and astonishing creation,

Fulton's sub could only descend twenty-five feet and carry four men, not a hundred. The original *Nautilus* moved by use of a screw propeller that had to be turned by hand, not via electric current. Not until the United States Navy's atomic submarine *Nautilus* came along in the 1950s was there any under-water craft remotely like the sub in *Twenty Thousand Leagues*. In his novel, Verne also created a new, improved diving suit without a bulky lifeline (as suits had in the 1870s) and with cylinders of oxygen attached. Ten years later such suits became a reality.

Despite all of his research, Jules made a few mistakes in his novel, which his brother, Paul would tease him about in later years. For one thing, although the *Nautilus* dips and dives, rams ships on the surface, and runs smack into icebergs, nothing on the sub is ever tied down. Yet only on one occasion is anything inside the submarine ever knocked over or displaced.

Twenty Thousand Leagues under the Sea actually took a while to catch on with the public. When it did, Verne knew he had to write a sequel clearing up the many mysteries of Nemo and the *Nautilus*, which was supposedly destroyed in a whirlpool at the end of the book. The sequel, called *The Mysterious Island* (1875), begins when several men escape from Richmond, Virginia, during the U.S. Civil War, by balloon. They include Captain Cyrus Harding (who serves under Grant), war correspondent Gideon Spilett, Harding's freed

Verne introduced the mysterious Captain Nemo of the submarine *Nautilus* in the best-selling book *Twenty Thousand Leagues under the Sea.*

ex-slave Neb, the sailor Pencroft, and his orphaned fifteen-year-old ward Herbert. Harding's dog, Top, comes along for good measure.

Blown off course by a storm, the balloon deposits its inhabitants on a seemingly deserted island. From the first, mysterious things happen that seem to indicate a guardian angel is watching over the men. Captain Harding is pulled unconscious from the sea while the others are indisposed and unable to help him, and Top is miraculously saved from a creature in a lake.

Building a home for themselves in the granite cliff, the castaways fight off a pirate attack. The unseen benefactor blows up the pirate ship. The guardian angel also helps when an army of apes tries to seize their "granite house" shelter.

This benefactor is eventually revealed to be Captain Nemo. The crippled *Nautilus* is in a grotto on the far side of the island. Nemo at last relates his personal history: He is really Prince Dakkar of India, whose wife and child were killed when the Indians rose up against British rule in the Sepoy revolt of 1857. When the Sepoys were overcome, Dakkar fled his country with a price on his head. Disgusted with the world, he gathered some comrades, went into hiding, and eventually became the notorious "Captain Nemo." It was British ships that the *Nautilus* fired upon in *Twenty Thousand Leagues*.

Verne also decided to use the opportunity to tie up a loose end from *The Children of Captain Grant*. A half-crazed man that the castaways find on another nearby island turns out to be Ayrton, Captain Grant's treacherous mate who had been banished there as punishment.

One of Verne's favorite childhood novels was Johann Rudolf Wyss's *Swiss Family Robinson*. He had always wanted to craft a contribution to "castaway/desert island" literature. *The Mysterious Island* was only the first of his stories in this genre. He even, many years later, wrote a sequel to *Swiss Family Robinson* using the same characters. Hetzel rejected the first version of Mysterious Island. "It's too silly," Hetzel wrote. "Where's the science? Cut it down by half and buck it up!"

In the revision, Verne tells the story of his Civil War castaways with real dramatic flair, but it is necessary to suspend disbelief over some elements of the novel. Cyrus Harding conveniently seems to know everything there is to know about engineering—and virtually everything else. None of the characters seem to miss or even think about the life they left behind, and they spend more time turning the island into a vacation paradise than they do in trying to get off of it.

But Verne was writing a survival adventure story, not a psychological drama. Philosophically, he believed that providential coincidences occurred everyday. Although he used science in his fiction, Verne remained a religious man who was convinced that God intervened in people's lives. He reflected this spiritual belief in his work through convenient plot turns. He also knew that readers would accept these things in his stories because they found them so entertaining and, due to Verne's painstaking research, realistic.

Verne also used *The Mysterious Island* to put forth his feelings about the American Civil War. He was clearly on the side of the Union and against slavery, as are the characters in the novel. Although the tone toward him is patronizing given the period, Neb is a very positively drawn black character. In his later Civil War novel *North against South* (1887), Verne's hero was an abolitionist, and his portraits of blacks are quite sympathetic.

Verne, and his fellow Frenchmen, had other things to worry about besides the U.S. Civil War. France was on the verge of a terrible war that would have dire consequences for the country and would throw the life of Jules Verne and his family into turmoil.

Chapter Seven

War

By the end of the 1860s, relations between Napoleon III of France, and Premier Bismarck of Prussia, who was determined to unify all the German states into one country, had deteriorated. War between Prussia and France seemed inevitable. Many citizens of France were anxious for war and convinced of victory.

Jules Verne had a more sober attitude. No matter who won—and it very likely would not be France—the war would take a terrible toll. "Let us not be too blind or too boastful," he said, "but rather recognize that one side is just as strong as the other, now that we fight with long-range weapons."

In July 1870, war broke out and Prussian troops began marching on France. Young men were drafted and sent to the front. Jules tried to reassure his family, but deep down he was worried. He learned that he was to be awarded the Legion of Honor, one of his nation's

highest honors, for his books, which had been translated into many languages and brought honor to France.
He took his family to Paris for the ceremony, then went
to Chantenay to see his parents and show them the
medal. It was during this reunion that he learned that
his government requested his help. Pierre Verne was
astonished that his son was being called to active military duty when he was forty-two years of age.

Jules was not being sent to the war front, however,
but back to Le Crotoy. He—and most importantly, his
boat *Saint Michel*—had been commissioned to orga-
nize a fleet of small boats to guard the coast. Twelve
soldiers were assigned to assist Jules in patrolling the
Somme Bay. Fortunately, the enemy never materialized.
The cannon, installed on his boat for defense, was "about
the size of a poodle" he noted. Jules spent most of his
time in the cabin working on his novels. He was away
from his family, who was staying with Honorine's parents in Amiens, for eight long months.

In the meantime, Prussian troops surrounded Paris,
but the proud city refused to surrender. Thousands of
Parisians died of hunger or from artillery fire. Finally,
after five months of siege, France surrendered to
Prussia. In the settlement, France lost possession of the
disputed territory of Alsace-Lorraine and was forced to
pay reparations to the enemy, which meant the French
people had to be heavily taxed. Worse still was the great
destruction in Paris.

When Jules finally was able to make his way to his publisher's office with new manuscripts, he found it empty. Most of Hetzel's employees had not yet returned from their war posts, and business had been so adversely affected Hetzel did not know if he could continue publishing.

Jules no longer had an income and his savings were running low. He considered going back to work in the stock exchange. His ailments returned as he worried about his future and his family. He considered moving in with his brother, Paul, who lived in Paris, while his family stayed with his in-laws. The Vernes economized as best they could. Jules finally decided there was nothing for him to do but to continue writing everyday and hope that his career had not come to a premature conclusion. One bright spot was the award he was given from the French Academy for *Twenty Thousand Leagues under the Sea.*

He wrote three novels during this bleak period. The one that brought him the greatest success was the amusing, rollicking adventure *Around the World in Eighty Days* (1872). *Around the World* is still well known and often read. Maybe because he knew he needed a crowd pleaser of a novel to reinvigorate his career, Verne was determined to amuse and thrill the reader and made the novel a real "page-turner." The pace is brisk and, unlike *Twenty Thousand Leagues*, the reader does not have to plow through pages and pages of research.

The protagonist, the strange—and strangely pre-cise—Phileas Fogg, is at first an unsympathetic charac-ter who eventually emerges as admirable and likable. His new manservant, Passepartout, is relishing the thought of how peaceful it will be working for a proper English gentleman when Fogg informs him that he will be accompanying his employer on a whirlwind trip around the world. Fogg has impulsively bet his life savings to prove to disbelieving associates at his club that a man can circle the globe in only eighty days. Meanwhile, a man fitting Fogg's description has robbed the Bank of England of fifty-five thousand francs. A wily detective, Fix, is convinced this trip around the world is only a ruse for Fogg to escape with the money. He makes up his mind to dog his every step.

The characters are chased by religious zealots in Bombay, rescue a woman who is about to be sacrificed to the Goddess Kali, and ride an elephant to Calcutta when it turns out the train tracks have not been com-pleted. In Hong Kong they are bushwhacked in an opium den. In San Francisco they are caught in a riot that has erupted over the election of the justice of the peace. The train they take to cross the American West is attacked by Sioux Indians and barely makes it over a trestle before it collapses.

When the ship in which they are sailing back to England moves too slowly, Fogg simply buys it and has it practically dismantled in mid-ocean. Fogg and

Passepartout believe they have arrived back in England a day too late before learning they have gained a day in their travels by crossing time lines so often. They barely make it to the club at the appointed hour to celebrate their victory. It turns out that Fogg and the bank robber are not the same person.

Around the World in Eighty Days was just the diversion that the French needed after the tragedy

Adventurer Nellie Bly bested Verne's *Around the World in Eighty Days* by completing the trip in seventy-two days.

of the Franco-Prussian war. First serialized in the magazine *Temps* (*Time*), it became an immediate sensation. A highly successful theatrical adaptation soon followed and ended his money worries forever. Ironically, Jules did not like the play. "The first half of the evening the audience is longing for the elephant to appear," he said, "and the rest of the evening they are regretting that they won't see it again!"

Jules had almost single handedly saved the Hetzel publishing firm. It was a time of glorious triumph and he would have been the happiest man on earth had he not received news around this time that his father had passed away. While Pierre Verne may at first have objected to Jules's writing, he eventually became his son's biggest booster, something that the grieving Jules would always remember.

For his next, and most grotesque, novel, Verne was influenced by true stories of famous shipwrecks, including the British *Sarah Sands* in 1857. The painting *The Wreck of the Medusa* also stimulated his imagination. This work by Gericault, which hung in the Louvre in Paris, depicted a French ship wrecked off the coast of Africa in 1816.

The Chancellor (1875) is not only one of Verne's greatest novels, but probably the best of his non-fantastic works. It is a harrowing, suspenseful, unremitting tale of the horror and desperation experienced by the survivors of a shipwreck. The trouble begins when spontaneous combustion erupts in a shipment of cotton stored in the ship's hold. Despite the best efforts of the first mate, the *Chancellor* must be abandoned. Eighteen people wind up on a makeshift raft in the middle of the ocean. The survivors include the narrator, Mr. Kazallon; the petroleum king, Mr. Kear, and his sickly wife; the ill woman's companion, Miss Herbey; the crippled twenty-year-old Andre Letourneur, and his doting father; and Jynxstrop, a troublesome cook who stirs up the other sailors.

Verne is unrelenting in his descriptions of the terrible suffering the survivors endure. A great storm washes two of the sailors overboard; the food runs out on New Year's Day. Some of their water turns out to have been accidentally poisoned. The sailors threaten to mutiny, and gnawing hunger nearly drives everyone crazy. Kazallon drinks his own blood at one point by opening a vein with his knife. Large sharks appear and devour Jynxstrop when he dives overboard in a fit of madness. The castaways finally spot a ship in the distance, but it never sees them. They sink to the very depths of despair.

The most shocking detail of the ordeal is the descent into cannibalism that develops as the survivors become more and more hungry. First there are the ominous remarks made by some of the sailors. When a young lieutenant passes away, it is discovered that someone has cut off his right foot during the night and used it for bait. Hobart, one of the sailors, turns out to have been hoarding food. After he commits suicide, the other sailors feast upon his flesh. Horrified, Kazallon and the other passengers refuse to partake of this gruesome meal.

In the novel's most chilling sequence, the sailors stare at the passengers and it is clear what they are thinking. The finale is a powerful sequence as the starving sailors force the others to draw lots to determine who will be butchered and eaten next. Miss Herbey begs everyone to wait one more day before killing the chosen man, Letourneur, with a hatchet. The next day Letourneur offers to let them hack off his arms so they can have something to feed upon. He is saved from this grisly fate when the castaways realize they are close enough to the coast to wait for rescue.

Unlike other novels by Verne, *The Chancellor* has no comedic relief to lighten the tension. A well-written work, it carries the reader along with its vivid descriptions and compelling prose from the very first page and is in some ways the forerunner of the twentieth century "disaster" novel.

The shrimp boat that Jules named after his son had long since been replaced by a larger sea-going craft. Now with the success of *Around the World*, Jules had enough money to buy an even bigger boat that he dubbed the *Michel III*, an elegant yacht with a large saloon, dining room, pantry, galley, crew's quarters, and plenty of bunks. Jules and his family sailed along the coast of Africa in 1876 and then to Norway and Scotland the following year.

Jules next wrote his greatest historical novel, *Michael Strogoff* (1876). The title character is one of the couriers of the czar of Russia. He has been entrusted with a letter from the czar to the czar's brother, the grand duke, who resides in Siberia. Afraid that spies working for the Tartars who are plundering Russia will seize the letter if they learn who he is, Michael travels across frozen, desolate areas in disguise. In one heartrending scene, he must deny his own mother, whom he was not seen in three years, to protect his identity. She, in turn, is threatened with a whipping unless she admits he is her son. In anguish, Michael reveals his true identity to spare her and is blinded on orders of his archenemy, the miserable traitor Ivan Ogareff. This does not prevent him from making his tortuous way to his final destination with the aid of a young woman who had befriended his mother.

In the harrowing scenes depicting Tartar outrages against Russian citizens, Verne was no doubt calling upon his memories of Prussian attacks on his own countrymen. The climactic Tartar attack upon the grand duke's castle and the town surrounding it is reminiscent of the Prussian siege of Paris and the refusal of its citizens to surrender no matter what the cost.

Jules did not usually enjoy big parties, so his wife Honorine must have organized the fancy dress ball for eight hundred guests that the Vernes threw in 1877. The guests were told to come dressed as characters from his novels. There were undoubtedly more Phileas Foggs and Captain Nemos in the crowd than cannibalistic sailors from *The Chancellor*.

Honorine was recovering from an illness and had a relapse while preparing for the party. Her daughter Suzanne presided over the affair while Suzanne's husband donated his blood for a transfusion for his mother-in-law. "A unique event in human history," Jules joked, "A man offering his blood to save his mother-in-law." The Vernes held another, smaller party in 1885 and dressed as innkeepers. Honorine was in the best of health this time.

Jules's next work was an outlandish piece of science fiction entitled *Hector Servadac* (1877). The title character is a French captain stationed in Algeria, who is scheduled to fight a duel with a Russian count. Before the duel can take place, an earthquake rocks the world and strange things begin to happen. A lessening in the force of gravity, for example, allows Servadac and others in the area to jump much higher than before. They soon learn that most of the rest of the world has simply vanished and the new globe is only two thousand miles in circumference.

The secret is that Servadac and his companions are no longer on the earth, but on a fragment of it which a comet has skimmed off. After a series of long adventures, the comet's orbit takes it back toward the earth. Using a balloon to fly from the comet to the earth at just the right moment, Servadac and company return unharmed, their chunk of earth pretty much back in the same spot where it was originally.

The novel has an original, even absurd, plot that Verne bolsters with strong dollops of contemporary science. He must have realized that if a terrestrial body were to strike our planet even a glancing blow the result would be utter catastrophe. He also knew that it was impossible for anyone to survive the transfer from comet to earth or vice versa. But Verne often winked at his readers and expected them to go along with his imagination for the sake of the story.

An odious aspect of *Hector Servadac* is the depiction of a Jewish peddler and skinflint named "Dutch Isaac," who is a blatant anti-Semitic stereotype that was not unusual in literature of the period. It has been suggested that Verne was upset over a controversy that had haunted him for the rest of his life. When Verne had heard of an absurd rumor that he was secretly a Polish Jew who had hid his faith in the hopes of marrying a wealthy Polish woman, he initially had a good laugh and jokingly related that he had actually kidnapped the woman but she had committed suicide. To his dismay, however, this ludicrous tall tale was seized upon as fact by some and proved to be resistant to the truth.

Whatever the cause of the characterization of Dutch Issac in the book, his American publishers decided to either change Isaac's ethnic background, or to alter the ending so that he is revealed to be a sympathetic character. Perhaps in response to this negative reaction, one of the most sympathetic characters in his later novel *The Carpathian Castle* (1892) is a Jewish innkeeper.

Now middle-aged and exhausted from his ceaseless work, Verne had written most of the books that became world-famous. But the prolific writer had many more stories to tell.

Chapter Eight

Creativity and Twilight

Jules Verne wrote over sixty books in his lifetime. Although he no longer needed to keep working in order to support his family, or to keep his name in front of the public, stories continued to pour from his pen. He was a consummate storyteller, and as long as he had stories to tell, he would write. The quality may have diminished— most critics felt that he wrote these later books too quickly—but the quantity seldom slacked.

In the 1880s, Verne published such novels as *The Giant Raft* (1881), in which an entire village is carried down the Amazon, and *The Green Ray* (1882), about a light that allowed one to be lucky in love. *The Southern Star Mystery* (1884) was set in the diamond mines of South Africa, and *Matthias Sandorf* (1885) concerns a man who escapes prison and revenges himself upon his betrayers.

Just as he had invented a fantastic fictional submarine in *Twenty Thousand Leagues*, he did the same for helicopters in *Clipper of the Clouds* (1886) and its sequel *Master of the World* (1904). Inventor Robur is sneered at for his enormous heavier-than-air flying machine, but has the last laugh when he uses it to rescue the once-snickering scientists now imperiled in their lighter-than-air machine. Verne's craft, the *Albatross*, not only foreshadows the modern helicopter, but also is built of plastic. In the second book, the machine can also zip along the ground and cruise under the water. These books created a new genre of "air warfare" fiction.

In his later years, Verne continued to travel. In 1884, the Verne family went on a second cruise on the *Michel III*. His brother, Paul, and nephew Gaston joined Honorine and Michel as they sailed to the Mediterranean and visited such places as Lisbon, Gibraltar, Algiers, and Malta. Their final destination was Italy, where Jules received an audience with Pope Leo XIII in Rome. The pope told him that it was not the scientific knowledge in his books that most impressed him, but the moral and spiritual values that they expressed. In Venice, Jules tried to remain incognito, but a proud Honorine told everyone who he was and a huge celebration ensued. Jules slipped away and went to bed early while the guests continued to party. Honorine was sick of sailing, however, due to inclement and dangerous weather and insisted they return to France by train.

Two years later, Jules learned from his brother, Paul, that his nephew Gaston had suffered a nervous breakdown. Gaston had been working for the Ministry of Foreign Affairs and the official story was that he was overworked. But Gaston appeared to have serious psychological problems. Paul hired nurses to watch over him and prevent him from leaving the house. One of Gaston's bizarre fixations was that the French public did not appreciate his Uncle Jules enough. Others thought Gaston might be jealous of his famous uncle.

Jules and his family permanently relocated to Amiens. In March 1886, Gaston escaped from his nurses and fled with one of his father's revolvers. He managed to get on a train to Amiens and made his way to his uncle's house. Jules was returning from the library when Gaston jumped out of the bushes near the front door and shot him in the leg. Jules wrestled the gun away from the young man, then collapsed in agony as neighbors rushed to his aid. Gaston explained that he thought killing his uncle would bring the "unappreciated" Jules Verne the honor he deserved.

For years, Verne's family and its descendants tried to cover up that his assailant had been Gaston. Family tension and strife were not uncommon in the family. Jules's relationship with his own son was occasionally troubled; he even had Michel arrested at one point after a bitter and violent quarrel. Jules was overjoyed when Michel finally settled down and got married.

The Vernes moved to a house in Amiens, Honorine's hometown, in 1886. Jules is standing on the left with his dog. Honorine is in the doorway.

It took many months for Jules to recover from the attack, and he was lame for the rest of his life. This dreadful incident was followed in rapid succession by the death of his mother, and the death of his friend and publisher, Pierre-Jules Hetzel. By this time, Hetzel's son, also named Jules, had taken over the business. Verne sold the *Michel III* when he realized that he had lost his "sea legs" and no longer enjoyed sailing. Then his beloved brother, Paul, died.

Jules sought refuge from life's trials in his work. He returned once again to the castaway genre inspired by his love of *Swiss Family Robinson*. As he had first read and loved Wyss's novel in childhood, Jules decided to write this new book for children aged ten to fourteen so they could experience the same thrill. It was his only story written specifically for juveniles. Verne has often been mislabeled a writer for children because of the fantastic nature of much of his material. Although young readers can and certainly have enjoyed Verne's novels over the years, most of his books were actually written with the adult reader in mind.

A Long Vacation (1888) concerns fourteen school-boys from New Zealand who are shipwrecked on a deserted island. A power struggle ensues between the arrogant English Doniphan, the forthright Bostonian Gordon, and the brave French boy Briant (whom Verne based on a classmate of his son's who later became secretary of foreign affairs). When he fails to be made

Verne was elected to serve on the Amiens municipal council in 1888.

leader, Doniphan gathers a few sycophants and breaks off from the rest of the boys. When Briant saves his life from an attacking jaguar, however, Doniphan gratefully offers him his friendship.

In the book's most thrilling sequence, the castaways build a giant kite so that they can see miles in each direction. Brave Briant rides the winds in an attached gondola. At the climax, the boys defend themselves in a bloody fight with guns and the cannon from the ruins of their boat when a gang of cutthroats attacks. Emerging victorious from the battle, they repair the cutthroats' boat and set sail from the island. A steamer bound for Australia eventually picks them up. Years later, William

Golding's masterpiece *Lord of the Flies* was also about schoolboys stranded on an island, but its tone is much darker.

In the late 1880s, Jules served on the municipal council of Amiens, though his election caused some controversy. He was considered a liberal, but ran on a conservative ticket, which greatly upset his wife. Some townspeople thought he would add prestige to the council; others thought he should stick with his writing. He was sincerely interested in the council's various social services and cultural activities and focused on improving the lot of the assorted traveling entertainers who came to Amiens. This civic experience led to his writing one of his most exciting and entertaining later works.

César Cascabel (1890) begins in the United States in 1867 and concerns a traveling circus troupe. The members of the troupe include the forty-five-year-old César Cascabel, his wife, Cornelia, his daughter, Napoleone, his sons, Jean and Alexandre, and their employee, Clou. The family also travels with two horses, two dogs, a parrot, and a monkey named John Bull, which is a swipe by Cascabel who hates all things British.

Having amassed enough money to travel back to France, César buys a strongbox to keep his cash in, but the box is stolen by British farm hands and César has to rethink his plans. He cannot afford tickets to cross the ocean, so decides to make his way back to France in his

Jules Verne, 1904

wagon, the Belle Roulette. The family plans to cross the Bering Strait and work their way to Europe across Siberia and Russia. Along the way, a Russian refugee and a young Indian girl, Kayette, who is hoping to find work as a servant, join the family.

Cascabel and his family experience many adventures. At one point they find themselves adrift on an ice floe after a crevasse opens under the horses' feet. Kayette and Jean drift off on a separate chunk, and there is constant danger from icebergs and from the suffocating snow. In a particularly exciting scene, hundreds of voracious wolves attack the caravan and César has to set them on fire to save his family. When a sinister gang threatens the Cascabels, César comes up with a brilliant scheme to foil their plans. He convinces the gang members to play the villains in a production of *The Brigands of the Black Forest* first. During the production, he has them captured by a horde of Cossacks.

Other titles Jules worked on during the 1890s include *Mistress Branican* (1891), which was inspired by the story of his long-ago schoolteacher whose husband went to sea and never returned. He also completed an open-ended Edgar Allen Poe story as *The Mystery of Arthur Gordon Pym* (1897) and wrote a satire, *Propeller Island* (1895), about an island that can move around as if it were a boat.

Some of Verne's later titles were dismissed by the critics as being rushed and inferior to his earlier works.

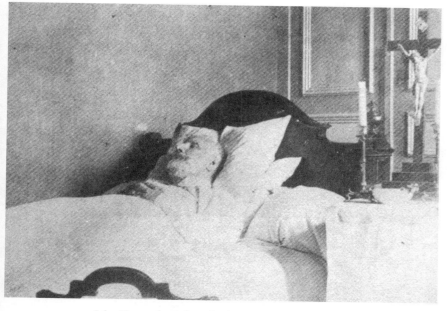

Jules Verne, the father of science fiction, died in 1905.

Some were even rejected for translation by American and English publishers. But each of his books retained fascinating aspects. In *The Village in the Treetops* (1901), Verne employed the idea of a new race "intermediate between the most advanced of the apes and the lowest men." Ironically, in a sense he made use of a kind of a "missing link," even though as a Catholic he rejected Darwin's theory of evolution. In his search for new, exciting stories based on recent scientific discoveries and theories, Verne clearly was not limited by his personal beliefs. Several other books, such as the gold rush adventure *The Golden Volcano* (1906), and the psychological thriller *The Secret of Wilhelm Storitz* (1910), were published posthumously.

In his later years, Jules Verne suffered numerous ailments. His leg injury troubled him for the rest of his life. He developed serious writer's cramp, began losing his hearing, and developed cataracts on his eyes. He suffered from diabetes, which was mostly untreatable, and the symptoms became progressively worse. He suffered a stroke when he was seventy-seven that paralyzed his entire right side. Honorine hired a nurse to help take care of him. Before long, the paralysis spread over his whole body and affected his brain. He no longer recognized his wife or son and soon slipped into a coma. At eight in the morning on March 24, 1905, Jules Verne breathed his last and went off on what may have been his greatest adventure.

Sculptor Albert Roze created a special statue of Verne that was placed over his tomb in the Cemetery de la Madeleine at Amiens. It shows Verne rising from his grave, with one arm reaching toward the stars. A plague reads: "ONWARD TO IMMORTALITY AND ETERNAL YOUTH." Through his stories, which have delighted readers of all ages for generations, Jules Verne has truly become immortal.

Chapter Nine

The Legacy of Jules Verne

After Verne's death, a massive bronze safe was passed on to his son, Michel, and stayed in the family until it came into the possession of his great-grandson, Jean Verne. The safe was never opened, weighed half a ton, and had no key. Jean decided to open it and hired a specialist in explosives to blow the heavy door off the safe. Inside was a long-lost handwritten manuscript of the unpublished novel *Paris in the Twentieth Century*.

Scholars had known of the novel's existence for years, and often wondered why it had never been published. They assumed it had been written when Jules was very old, and his handwriting indecipherable. We now know that *Paris in the Twentieth Century* was written early in Verne's career.

After the manuscript was authenticated, it was published in France in 1994 and sold over one hundred thousand copies. Ninety years after his death, Jules

Verne was back on the bestseller list. The book was quickly translated into English and published in the United States.

Hetzel, who had rejected the manuscript in 1864, had scribbled in the margin of the manuscript: "If you were a prophet, no one today would ever believe your prophecies."

In *Paris in the Twentieth Century,* Verne forecasts automobiles, gas stations, elevators, computers, pollution, fax machines, and giant chain book stores whose clerks are unfamiliar with the great writers of the past. He also forecasted electric streetlights, atonal and electronic music, and elevated railways with trains that run on compressed air and electromagnetic force. The world of the "future" that he describes is one in which rents are impossibly high (certainly true today in major cities like Paris and New York), France is owned and controlled by foreign interests, and technology is so dominant that art and culture are appreciated only by the very few.

Paris in the Twentieth Century was a surprise to those who thought Jules Verne had always blindly championed scientific progress. Actually, in such works as *The Begum's Fortune* (1879) and *Topsy Turvey* (1889), Verne wrote of men who used technology irresponsibly or for outright evil purposes. He undoubtedly agreed with Abraham Lincoln's comment that "true progress lies in man's heart." But Jules Verne has always been misunderstood. This is due to a great extent because of the often poor translations and film adaptations of his work. One British translator, Edward Roth, even took it upon himself to rewrite the books the way Verne supposedly would have written them if he had been American.

Hollywood began adapting Verne's stories during the silent movie period. The film *20,000 Leagues under the Sea* (1916) combined that novel with its sequel, *The Mysterious Island,* into one movie. It reveals that Nemo is actually a prince from India, but gives him a grown daughter who somehow winds up on the island with the castaways. The full-color 1954 version features a superb performance by James Mason as Nemo, but turns Ned Land, played by Kirk Douglas, into a bumpkin. There have been other versions made for television, but only the 1954 film, while taking liberties with the story, is a genuinely memorable motion picture.

Another version of *The Mysterious Island* in 1961 has Nemo experimenting with gigantism on the island and creating monstrous crabs and other creatures that threaten the castaways. Ruins from Atlantis (as in *Twenty Thousand Leagues*) are conveniently located near the island.

The advertising campaign for the film version of *Around the World in Eighty Days* (1956) cemented the association of Jules Verne with balloons in the public's mind. Posters for the film depicted a scene in which

Fogg and Passepartout ride in a balloon—a scene that never occurs in the novel. Otherwise the film is faithful to the book in plot and spirit.

Most of Verne's novels have been turned into films and television series. Unfortunately, most were forgettable. Countless writers and filmmakers, however, have been influenced by Verne's stories, and so have a great number of individuals in other professions. These include scientists, inventors, and engineers, such as Konstantin Tsiolkovski, William Beebe, Simon Lake, Wernher von Braun, Robert H. Goddard, Guglielmo Marconi and Hermann Oberth; explorers such as Norbert Casteret and Admiral Richard Byrd; and astronauts Yuri Gargarin and Neil Armstrong. Their love of Verne's stories of trips to the moon, the center of the earth, and the North Pole helped shaped the course of their lives. A mini-series about American efforts to reach the moon produced by actor Tom Hanks even borrowed Verne's title *From the Earth to the Moon.*

Astonishing fantasy tales were nothing new when Jules Verne began writing. The stories from Greek mythology were taught to every school child. The amazing voyages of Sindbad, and other, equally far-fetched folk tales from many different cultures were well known. But these earlier stories were fantasies that made no attempt to ground the creator's imagination in science. Jules Verne's contribution to literature was to attempt to imagine fantastic stories as if they were really *possible.*

He joined fantasy with well-researched speculation and, in turn, became the Father of Science Fiction, although that genre was not named until after his death.

Verne has often been compared with British author H.G. Wells, who also wrote fantastic stories. Wells's novels were excellent, but he admitted that his tales did not "pretend to deal with possible things." After reading Wells's novel *First Men in the Moon* (1901), Verne commented that Wells did not even try to come up with a reasonable explanation for the trip as he had in *From the Earth to the Moon*. "He constructs [a] metal which does away with the law of gravitation," Verne complained. "That's all very well, but show me this metal. Let him produce it."

Many of Jules Verne's novels are still in print, and readers continue to be fascinated and intrigued by his novels of scientific speculation and frenzied suspense. He was one of the first fiction writers to become world famous. Today, many novels and movies owe a debt to the talent and imagination of the dreamer from Nantes.

Major Works

1863—Five Weeks in a Balloon
1864—A Journey to the Center of the Earth
1865—From the Earth to the Moon
1866—The Adventures of Captain Hatteras (Part One: At the North Pole; Part Two: The Wilderness of Ice)
1868—The Children of Captain Grant
1870—Around the Moon; Twenty Thousand Leagues under the Sea
1871—A Floating City
1873—Around the World in Eighty Days
1875—The Mysterious Island; The Chancellor
1876—Michael Strogoff
1877—Black Diamonds; Hector Servadac (Part One: To the Sun; Part Two: Off On a Comet)
1879—The Begum's Fortune
1881—The Giant Raft (Part One: The Giant Raft; Part Two: The Cryptogram)
1882—The Green Ray
1884—The Southern Star Mystery

1885—Matthias Sandorf
1886—The Clipper of the Clouds
1887—North Against South
1888—A Long Vacation
1889—Topsy Turvey: A Family without a Name
1890—César Cascabel (Part One: The Traveling Circus; Part Two: The Show on Ice)
1891—Mistress Branican
1892—Carpathian Castle
1895—Propeller Island
1896—For the Flag
1897—The Mystery of Arthur Gordon Pym
1900—Their Island Home: The Later Adventures of the Swiss Family Robinson
1901—The Village in the Treetops
1904—Master of the World
1905—The Lighthouse at the End of the World
1906—The Golden Volcano
1910—The Secret of Wilhelm Storitz
1994—Paris in the Twentieth Century (written 1863)

Sources

CHAPTER ONE: "IN MY IMAGINATION"

p. 13, "Studious children . . ." I.O. Evans, *Jules Verne and His Work* (London: Arco, 1965), 20.

p. 17 "in my imagination . . ." Catherine O. Peare, *Jules Verne: His Life* (New York: Holt, Rinehart and Winston, 1956), 36.

CHAPTER TWO: PARIS

p. 25, "Infernal politics . . ." Peare, *His Life*, 53.

p. 28, "I am going to devote . . ." Ibid., 51.

CHAPTER THREE: STRUGGLING

p. 34, "What I need . . ." Evans, *Verne and His Work*, 31.

p. 35, "better at banter . . ." Peare, *His Life*, 71.

CHAPTER FOUR: BALLOONING

p. 46, "Boys, I'm leaving . . ." Evans, *Verne and His Work*, 41.

p. 49, "a fool . . . and a ninny" Eugene Weber, "Introduction" to *Paris in the Twentieth Century* (Random House: New York, 1996) ixv.

p. 50, "petty journalism," Fred Coleman, "Prophet Scorned," *U.S. News and World Report* Vol. 117, issue 13 (November 10, 1994): 16.

CHAPTER FIVE: REMARKABLE JOURNEYS

p. 56, "inside a liquid core . . ." Michael Ko, "Sorry, Jules Verne . . ." *Chicago Tribune* (December 13, 1998)

p. 58, "Play Adam to some daughter . . ." Evans, *Verne and His Work*, 49.

CHAPTER SIX: CELEBRITY

p. 62, "I start by making . . ." Marie Belloc, "Jules Verne at Home," *The Strand* (February 1895)

p. 63, "I do not seem . . ." Ibid.

p. 64, "Hardly here . . ." Evans, *Verne and His Work*, 59.

p. 71, "It's too silly . . ." Jean H. Guermonprez, "The Works of Jules Verne," *French Literary Review* (May/June 1955)

CHAPTER SEVEN: WAR

p. 73, "Let us not be too blind . . ." Peare, *His Life*, 56.

p. 74, "about the size . . ." Evans, *Verne and His Work*, 68.

p. 77, "The first half of the evening . . ." Ibid., 71.

p. 81, "A unique event . . ." Ibid., 76.

CHAPTER EIGHT: CREATIVITY AND TWILIGHT

p. 93, "intermediate between . . ." Evans, *Verne and His Work*, 133.

CHAPTER NINE: THE LEGACY OF JULES VERNE

p. 96, "If you were a prophet . . ." Cynthia Sanz and Cathy

Nolan, "The Family Jules," *People* Vol. 43, Issue 6 (February 13, 1995): 183.

p. 99, "pretend to deal . . ." "Introduction" by H.G. Wells to his *Collected Scientific Romances*.

Glossary

antediluvian: before the great flood or deluge; ancient
bohemian: belonging to a group of people who are unconventional and generally artistic
Cossacks: Russian military horsemen
cryptography: writing in secret characters or code
divertissement: an entertaining diversion
eradicate: to thoroughly destroy
erudite: learned and scholarly
"eternal triangle": situation in which, for instance, a man loves a woman, but she loves another man.
hempen: made of the tough fibers of the hemp plant, used for rope, etc.
patronizing: to act kindly to one you feel superior to
propensity: a natural inclination
propitious: affording favorable conditions or circumstances
risqué: off-color; improper
seismologist: scientist who studies earthquakes
spelunker: cave explorer
sycophant: a fawning flatterer
Tartars: violent tribes that attacked Russia; savage people

thespian: actor
trenchant: clearly and sharply defined
vitiate: to spoil, pollute, blunt the effect
voracious: greedily hungry

Bibliography

Allott, Kenneth. *Jules Verne*. London: Arco, 1940.

Clarke, Arthur C. "Introduction" to *From the Earth to the Moon* and *Around the Moon*. New York: Dodd, Mead and Company, 1962.

Coleman, Fred. "Prophet Scorned." *U.S. News and World Report*, November 3, 1994.

Emerson, Tony and Hideko Takagama. "Jules Verne, Explorer." *Newsweek*, July 5, 1993.

Evans, Arthur B. and Ron Miller. "Jules Verne, Misunderstood Visionary." *Scientific American*, April 1997.

Evans, I.O. *Jules Verne and His Work*. London: Arco, 1965.

Paris, Michael. "Air Warfare." *History Today*, Vol. 43, June 1993, 29.

Peare, Catherine O. *Jules Verne: His Life*. New York: Holt, Rinehart, and Winston, 1956

Sanz, Cynthia and Cathy Nolan. "The Family Jules." *People*, February 13, 1995.

Schoell, William. "The Making of *Journey to the Center of the Earth*." *Filmfax*, No. 55, March/April 1996.

Taves, Brian and Stephen Michaluk Jr. *The Jules Verne Encyclopedia.* Lanham, Md.: Scarecrow Press, 1996.

Weber, Eugene. "Introduction" to *Paris in the Twentieth Century.* New York: Random House, 1996.

Websites

The Jules Verne Collection Website by Andrew Nash:
http://www.julesverne.ca/

Garmt de Vries' Jules Verne Collection:
http://www.phys.uu.nl/~gdevries/verne/verne.html

Musée Jules Verne of Nantes, France: (Website is in French)
http://www.nantes.fr/mairie/services/responsabilites/dgc/
julesverne/

Zvi Har'El's Jules Verne Collection: Links to Jules Verne
related sites
http://jv.gilead.org.il/

Index